IN THE SPACES BETWEEN STARS LIE SHADOWS

© John Bartlett 2024

All rights reserved. Except for appropriate use in a book review, no part of this publication may be reproduced, stored in a retrieval system, or transmitted in any form or by any means, without the prior permission of the publisher, or in the case of photocopying or reprographic copying, a licence from the Copyright Agency of Australia.

John Bartlett has asserted his right under the Copyright, Designs and Patents Act 1988 to be identified as the author of this work.

Cover image: KRISTAS UNGURS (Pexels, free selection)

IN THE SPACES BETWEEN STARS LIE SHADOWS

ISBN 9781763653061

Walleah Press
South Launceston
Tasmania, Australia 7249

www.walleahpress.com.au
ralph.wessman@walleahpress.com.au

Walleah Press

IN THE SPACES BETWEEN STARS LIE SHADOWS

John Bartlett

Contents

Prevarication	1
We the endangered	2
light discontined	3
migratory restlessness	4
nature's bonfire burns on	5
learning how to die	6
Love and its penalties	7
a canticle of calm	8
about water	9
a crouching god	10
everywhere you look	11
reconstructed light	12
Four Poems	13
not one stone	14
Sonnet for Gareth	15
even if we want to love	16
questions about unnatural selection	17
notes on pruning and regrafting	18
although the missiles	19
on the advice of children	20
the risk litany	21
the last thylacine in Tasmania	22
remembering Terry	24
magpie song	25
a pianto	26
the spaces between stars	27
About the Author	28

Acknowledgements

Thanks to the editors of *The Crow, Q-Lit anthology 2024, Poetry Catalog, Ros Spencer Poetry Prize 2023, Allegro Poetry, Bluebottle, Cerasus magazine* and *London Grip* who have already published some of the poems in this collection.

I would also like to acknowledge that these poems were written on the unceded lands of the Wadawurrung and pay my respects to their Elders, past and present.

Previous publications

Towards a Distant Sea 2005 by Indra Publishing
All Mortal Flesh 2009 Heartsong Publishing
Estuary 2013 Heartsong Publishing
A Tiny and Brilliant Light 2017 Heartsong Publishing (ebook)
Jack Ferryman: Reluctant Private Eye Heartsong Publishing 2019 e-book
The Arms of Men 2019 Melbourne Poets Union
Songs of the Godforsaken 2019 Picaro Poets
Awake at 3am 2020 Ginninderra Press
Eschatology 2022 Picaro Poets
These Luminous Earth 2023 Picaro Poets
Excitations of Entanglement 2023 Ginninderra Press

PREVARICATIONS

I scrutinise the world intently
the street-shock surge
of crowds the outrage
of competing flags
air chant buzzing
hard times

we've become accustomed to
the halitosis of war
all its useless beauty
we're programmed for prevarications

I age like brittle parchment
only now have I learned
to live within the stretch
of a day's hours

inside my dreams I fall
like petals from
fading roses

for now I'm interested only
in pondering
the 26 neck bones
of a swan

WE THE ENDANGERED

for Stephen

I'm counting all the birds endangered
those little lorikeets
elastic, acrobatic, gymnastic
their lovely lurking in Melaleuca flowers
their nesting nooks in Moonah

the open plains of my childhood
are emptying now
the wooden hollows of honeysuckle shrinking
the roosting white-faced terns vanishing
this night peacock ululating
the swifting white-throated needletails diminishing

here by your hospital bed
I'm learning the lessons of vigil
from two plovers outside
those silent sentinels
teaching us survival in these unsacreds
how to be adroit at keeping watch

what is life but a foolish flame
of vanishings and disappearances
tiny flames flickering
until at last we can witness
those departing angels of
the Everbright
bearing us skyward

you know don't you
that you and I
have hardly been here

LIGHT DISCONTINUED

I love the almost-light
early morning gloom,
her shifting silences, all those
remnants of dreamdrag

shadows amorphous anonymous
soft enough to shape into promises of
hope, of virtues or even grace
if strong enough
to withstand daylight's harsh judgements

darkness is a quicksand
night is for murdering
and the taste of your mouth

MIGRATORY RESTLESSNESS

they cross borders we cannot cross
the North Star alone their compass
even caged birds know this stirring

when beginnings feel more like endings
when the Arctic summer arrives early
they cross borders we cannot cross

non-stop, star-struck, moon-bound
burning muscles that beat their wings
even caged birds know this stirring

the Eastern Curlew breeds in Russia's swamps
estuaries, harbours, lagoons & marshes
they cross borders we cannot cross

where once a wetlands nursery
now shrill steel and concrete's conceits
they cross borders we cannot cross
even caged birds feel this stirring

NATURE'S BONFIRE BURNS ON

– title from 'That Nature is a Heraclitean Fire
and of the comfort of the Resurrection' by
Gerard Manley Hopkins

Sometimes
the arching arrogance of
sea waves astounds

the mouth-frotted estuary
the mesh the mix of sea's mastery
the lugwormed Braille on beaches
the grinding shrill of stars travelling
all that unbeautiful flame-rage
in treetops

we do know that sometimes
earth's skin stretches
it breaks too
the wounding and the pain

but sometimes brokenness is
just love's way of enduring

LEARNING HOW TO DIE

"death is the last wonder" D. H. Lawrence

two herons and I sit in vigil
their wings folded love letters
here on creek edge, currents
drag us towards helpless

I'm imprinted by the weight of kisses
all those coupling passions of lonely
those yearnings for gardens with
boughs of perfumed roses arching
towards sunlight
the extravagances of small birds

I'm just the black swan of crucifixion
suspended in air shot through
with the pulse, the pitch
of chants Gregorian

when at last beat of heart
the soul expands
our gamma rays will surge
will sweep away
all those contradictions

each day I dig the earth
I plant
I learn each day
new lessons in the
art of dying

LOVE AND ITS PENALTIES

when we were younger we
were rivers   raging desires smashing
against the rocks of proper
cavalier about destinations

like professional tourists on
endless mystery flights somehow now
still the beginnings, the 'not there yets'
with no end to our constant yearnings

I'm auditing my misdemeanours
with men   all that prowling the corridors
of lonely   so many anonymous kisses

I now know how many moons
has Jupiter   it's the adhesive
human heart that's so unfathomable

A CANTICLE OF CALM

this morning has broken open
with a scattering of wrens

a heron on black rocks
a tanker on the horizon

heading somewhere else
creek flowing softly

lugworms mapping a washed beach
surfers hesitating on stilled sea like

acolytes pausing prayers to you
the earth becoming pagan again

ABOUT WATER

    – after Mary Oliver

I wonder about water
    the shape of it,
        the sounds
            of its silences

one moment smooth
    – glistening voices
        singing songs of salvation
            then curling around

embracing smooth stones
    'til it leaps up
        in fright at
            the edges of high cliffs

then rushes downward
    resigned to its fate
        there's a spirit in water
            that's sometimes in me

A CROUCHING GOD

time is broken
we breathe in the essentials
leaking years seeping
into the deep down
earth dark

nights we sleep
in single beds
side by side like
drawers of cutlery

we know that graves
cannot hold those
who love excessively
or who ask where
stars go in daylight

oh the miracle and the mysteries
those clashing cymbals that
electrify our blood, urge us
to abandon these collapsing walls
of composted lies

ours is a crouching god with scars

EVERYWHERE YOU LOOK

this afternoon the birds gather
intent on long lingering

parrots in the salty light
turtledoves ogling the seed bowl

all queuing politely until
crows arrive with their dark desires

the honeyeater selects geranium flowers
not so choosy now it's winter

I walk to the estuary, listen to
the creek carrying its stories

where do these untold stories go
but into the ocean vastness

each moment is such a small thing
in the midst of these millennia

but no less beautiful, precious
precise and belongs to me

soon the winter bulbs will break through
with their green insistence

and as I wait for first flowers
I know now these moments,
this life, this place will be enough

RECONSTRUCTED LIGHT

on rain-drenched streets
glassy and perilous with pity

they shuffled towards their deaths
a father's arm around his daughter

as doors were closing behind them
they threw off their bodygarb

followed the footprints of lives past
limbs programmed for tyrant stories

they transferred to higher states
impatient now for heavensight

we are counted not by numbers
but the names
our mothers called us

FOUR POEMS

the swan curled on her nest
a question mark in repose
ducks shelter from nearby hunters

summer has come too early
plum blossom hangs pink and engorged
Hawaiian island wildfire death toll jumps

a bunch of poppies on a table
petals are butterfly wings unfolding
my mother always burned the stems

from palliative care he said
I'm dying while on the coastal track
the usual carpet of scattering wrens

NOT ONE STONE

      – after Mark Ch. 13 v. 25

these days the sky appears in shreds
stars fall down like leaves
your tears will not
prevent the bullying insistence

of sea rise, the fauna queuing
for Extinction, we've entered days
of Mogadon Dreaming, lighting candles
to the absent gods of fire and flood

when will we see this Earth renewed by
the startle of a thousand parrots
lifting up from overflowing waterholes
our hearts expanding as we
scroll back through time
to some unedited Eden still held in dusty vaults ?

SONNET FOR GARETH

you know all the mislaid sadnesses
live on in silences
all those small deaths
that disappoint us

this tightening planet with
its silky heart and
chafing skies so full of lies
our children walking backwards

but the moon is a living thing
rising and setting, melding and moulding
each small life

to be held by someone
celebrates the victory of
just breathing in and out
and in again

EVEN IF WE WANT TO LOVE...

so I ask the nesting swans
are we asleep or dreaming
or just in some state of deepdowness

does longing linger like love does
does it thicken the air as mist will
and what of desire's arrival, sudden
and arrogant around the borders of vigilance

I need uninterrupted stories of stars
to fill up the empty parts of me

though love may end in bitter
hunger and longing will endure
like prayers
and the searching necks
of Great Egrets

QUESTIONS ABOUT UNNATURAL SELECTION

What
      shall earth do
      with her children
      the motherless
      the fatherless
      all those surplus children

Who
      is there to embrace them
      when hearts break
      when continents wake

When
      they shift apart

What shall we do
      with all the orphan islands
      the predators, the parasites
      caught up in the drift
      of random selections

Will we still bear
      the gill slits
      of our fish forebears
      all the excess baggage of evolution
      the imprints of past crimes
      as now we drift closer
      to an upwelling
      of cosmic tenderness

NOTES ON PRUNING AND REGRAFTING

who will replant all the wounded trees
of Gaza and Ukraine and why

war on innocent leaves and branches
who then will shape a prayer

in this our voiceless air
the unlovely spaces of broken

after all the jagged pruning
what is left for perching birds

when spring breaks warless
when the owl turns toward the moon

when men learn to regraft tenderness
when gentleness goes viral

ALTHOUGH THE MISSILES

– after Adam Zagajewski

although the missiles still
rain down on Gaza
here light pauses at water's edge
wrens treading water in bird baths

although refugees still walk
away from the memories of their homes
a heron waits tenderly by the bridge &
pigeons preen mornings in the poplars

although children lie silent
in dusty hospital corridors &
the enemy is bulldozing our cemeteries
mothers light candles for soldier sons' return

although the gardens of tyrants
overflow with fragrant roses
a father cups the head of his newborn in wonder

the human heart it seems
is incapable of giving up on hope

ON THE ADVICE OF CHILDREN

the war in Gaza has been cancelled and
from the bombed out Kamal Adwan hospital
the children – amputees
or riddled with shrapnel –
sent out a communiqué
cancelling further hostilities
without further notice

we are many (they said)
and together with the returning dead
yet wrapped in the innocence of white
we will outnumber the men in suits
with microphones and missiles

then the children of Ukraine
called a press conference to announce
an embargo on missiles inscribed with our names
                        without further notice

the men in suits fell silent because
the profit margin on the sale of children's toys
is so much less than on missiles
remember you have (the children said)
but three score year and ten to live
and like the grasses you will wilt and die

we are the forever children
with eternities to wait and

                no further correspondence
                will be entered into (they said)

THE RISK LITANY

be not afraid to take a moment
to flirt with shadows
        to lie long nights
        in the arms of gamblers
go skating across the thin ice
of your lofty ambitions
        take a stroll on the high wire
        above anarchy
ride your bicycles into the
boardrooms of venture capitalists
        bombard with placards
        the bedrooms of despots
throw your life down
like a reckless hand of poker
        entrust your life
        to tipsy executioners for
a life without risk is just
*noisy brass or clanging cymbal**
        a sofa with broken springs
        too difficult to get out of

    *1 Corinthians 13:1

THE LAST THYLACINE IN TASMANIA

it's not that we don't get extinction
remember that video of the last thylacine in Tasmania
        its caged pacing back and forth
        its stripes like whip-marks
haven't we lived the long histories of flagellations too
all the bruisebashings   skin scorched
with Kaposi Sarcoma   dark as
                tree bark after fire

what could we do then but cover
ourselves under quilts of leaflayer
stitched together by our names

we lay down our hospital bones
in wards of hopeful   fragile
like the stalks of wind-blown anigozanthos

        vulnerable   enraged
we joined the ranks of the endangered
sheltering in darkness with the northern quoll
        in the cracks and crevices of
desires
        echoing the night call of
        the eastern curlew

        we were the Gouldian grassfinch,
        the regent honeyeater
        the black-footed rock wallaby

can we call this planet earth
when they are gone

today I saw the painted-lady butterfly
trapped behind glass   the hooded plover
                         laying eggs at the edge of
tides

we all know how damaged is our planet
still full of longing and foreboding but
don't ask us to sympathise
                we've long lived the vocabulary
                the geometries of near extinction

REMEMBERING TERRY

for Terry Bourke (1944 – 2023)

the day you went away
what could the air do
but rush in to fill the empty spaces
all that wind-snap-slap
wind-shock wind-song

it drove the boats forward
it ate up the heavens the way
black cockatoos lift and slice the solid skies
it left traces of love laughter longing
all those fine arts of leaning towards
when your wing-tip touched
this earth's electric soul

for a moment we tasted
all the sweet sharp shocks
of our youth's imaginings
and disappointments
but was this enough
we asked
to gain the admiration
or perhaps the envy
of the sometimes skittish gods

MAGPIE SONG

wattlebirds wait for darkness
to loosen the dreams of children
for days to taste of peace

Dianella fibres like silk
strong enough to resist
the callous winds of winter

river redgums along the banks
of my childhood suffered
dumb rage of axe and saw

autumn dew drops from leaves' length clear
dear atonements of magpies' songs
slice the crisp air into a day full of sky

where is that untouched world
its birds wide-winging
cormorants their dottled dipping
scratching the surface
of mirrored creeks   where

A PIANTO

it's autumn
the sharp-tailed sandpipers
ache with the need of leaving
all those tiny darting commas
scribbled across estuary sands
northward hope-driven by their tomorrows

gone too the white-throated
needletails with their celestial chanting
these small and sacred mercies
that stitch our days together
until sorrows fray and warp
the selvage of all our years

unravelling into tears and
although you too have left us
please return safely to our hearts
where the blurred imprints
of your vanished existence are
blue-prints of our own resurrectings

THE SPACES BETWEEN STARS

– after Robert Gray

we suspect, don't we that
our shared stories fall
from spaces between stars
into this dunesweep walk
that is never still with
its endless scripting motion
messages of Marram grass

I could not contemplate abandoning
the hiddeness of middens
to walk away from this ocean
its tug and tow with stars
or the motion of the white-faced heron's
neck when walking, moving like a metronome

everywhere we witness the casual shedding
of skins this 'shifting of energies' as our lives
shatter into a thousand little pieces
fragments propelled alone
by lovelight's smoulder

About the Author

John Bartlett is the author of eleven books of fiction, non-fiction and poetry. His first poetry pamphlet *The Arms of Men* was published by MPU. He was winner of the 2020 Ada Cambridge Poetry Prize and his latest poetry collection is *Excitations of Entanglement*. (Ginninderra 2023).

Milton Keynes UK
Ingram Content Group UK Ltd.
UKHW020324101024
449483UK00017BA/100